We've Got It Made

Words of Encouragement and Tips For Living A Truly Happy Life

By Bo Shafer

This book would have never happened without the encouragement of Rick Kuhlman and the many, many hours of work put in by Eli Smith transcribing my ramblings!

Table of Contents

Bo-verbs/Bo-isms

Throughout my life, I've collected a lot of short phrases of wisdom and/or humor that I will use in my interactions with people, from speaking engagements to everyday conversations. Some of these phrases I made up myself, and some of them I may have heard from someone else at some point in time. I honestly can't remember where most of them came from, so I won't take credit for any of them.

My friends have nicknamed these phrases "Bo-verbs" or Bo-isms" and many have suggested that I put them in book form. So here are the ones I can remember (after all, I am 82 years old!) I will talk about some of these phrases in more depth later in the book.

"Success comes in cans; not in cannots."

"The only people who don't have time are dead."

"Don't die before you're dead."

"The people who have the most birthdays live the longest."

"Only one thing gets better with age—your Forgetter. It gets better every year."

"When I get to Heaven, the first thing God is going to say to me is, 'Bo, you've got 2 weeks to gain 20 pounds'! And if that's not Heaven, I don't know what is!"

"I've got it figured out—in Heaven, ice cream is going to be a vegetable, and M&M's are going to be diet pills!

"Blessed are the flexible, for they shall not be bent out of shape."

"We do what we have to do so that we can do what we want to do."

"There is a community in every town that has no problems and makes no mistakes. It's called a cemetery."

"If something is hard and you really don't want to do it, it's probably the right thing to do."

"Success doesn't make you happy. Happiness makes you successful."

"How you treat your parents is how you will be treated by your children."

"There is only one thing worse than your child leaving home—your child not leaving home."

"Never say 'I've got to go to work.' Say 'I get to go to work.'"

"We can neglect the ones we love the most to have the things we need the least."

"The older I get, the better I was."

"When it comes to marriage—if in doubt, chicken out. Don't marry someone because you think you can live with them. Marry them because you can't live without them."

"Problems can make you better or bitter— your choice."

"Are you a thermostat or a thermometer?"

"Are you humbly grateful, or are you grumbly hateful?"

"A fish gets caught because he doesn't keep his mouth shut."

"Work is hard. If it was easy, they'd call it play."

"Complaining is a habit—people will interrupt you while you're complaining to try to out complain you."

"Tomorrow is a mystery, yesterday is history, and today is a gift. That's why they call it the present."

"When you wake up in the United States, you are about to spend another day in paradise."

"We waste more water waiting on hot water than a large portion of the world has -- and theirs is dirty."

"Good health is guaranteed to be temporary. Spiritual health is guaranteed forever— think about it."

"If we spent as much time and effort on our spiritual health as we do on our physical health, our whole world would be better."

"The best thing a father can do for his children is to love their mother."

"Everyone is religious. Whatever controls your life is your religion."

"Don't envy what someone else has if you are not willing to do what they did to get it."

"When the sun comes out, it changes everything. When the Son comes out (in us), He changes everything."

"There's a big difference between knowing about God and knowing God."

"God has given us a physical piece of sunshine that we can touch with our finger—they're called teeth. A big smile changes everything!"

"We often forget what we should remember and remember what we should forget."

"With great privilege comes great responsibility."

"The best things in life aren't things."

"Don't focus on being blessed. Focus on being a blessing."

"If you're doing nothing to change it, that means whatever is happening has your approval."

"Stay away from negative people. They will have a problem with every solution."

"Trial and error is a good way to find a spiritual gift."

"Giving up is a final solution to a temporary problem."

"The only life you can enjoy is your own."

"Failure teaches us what not to do—which can be more important than knowing what to do."

Blessings

I'm So Dadgum Blessed, It's Almost Ridiculous

I quit complaining in 1983.

They say it takes four to six weeks to break a habit, and complaining is a habit that can be broken just like any other. It's not easy though. You can hardly start complaining about something before somebody interrupts you to out-complain you. If you can go four to six weeks without complaining, people will notice—I guarantee it.

"How you doing, buddy?" I asked the parking lot attendant on a beautiful day in downtown Knoxville.

It was the deep frown etched on the man's face that had compelled me to speak to him. You have one chance to make a first impression on someone, and this man had already made his. But then he responded by saying something I had never heard before.

"I was okay, but I got over it."

Now that is the dumbest thing I've ever heard, I thought.

Being much bigger than the man, I gently put my arm around him. "Can I ask you a few questions?" I asked.

"Well, yeah," he said uncertainly. "Are you an American?"

"Yeah," said the man. "Are you healthy?" "Yeah."

"Have you got a job?" "Yes."

"You got a wife?" "Yeah."

"Does she love you?" (I took a chance on that one!) "Yes."

"She healthy?" "Yeah."

"You got any children?"

"Yeah, I got three."

"They healthy?"

"Yeah, they are."

"You got a house?" "Yeah."

"Is it warm in the winter?" "Yes."

"Is it cool in the summer?" "Yeah."

"Is it dry in the rain?" "Yeah."

"You got a car?"

"Yeah," he said, grinning sheepishly. "I got three."

"You ever been on a trip?" "Yeah."

"You an American citizen?" "Yeah."

I smiled at the man. "Now I'm gonna ask you one more time. How are you doing?"

"Gosh," said the parking garage attendant. "I guess I got it pretty good, don't I?"

"You sure do, ole' buddy!" I said, clapping him on the back. "Now, I bet you could change the attitude of about fifty people every day when they come in here and ask you how you're doing. Don't come up with a dumb line like, 'I was okay but I got over it.' Look them in the eye with a smile on your face and say, 'I'm so dadgum blessed it's almost ridiculous.' And they'll look at you like you looked at me. It won't take but a minute for you to explain to them how good we've got it. Now let me ask you something else. What did you do to deserve to be born healthy?"

"Uh," said the man. "Nothing, I guess."

"And what did you do to deserve to have healthy children?"

"Nothing."

"And you just told me you were okay, but you got over it!" I said. "Now, you've changed your attitude. See if you can change somebody else's attitude too."

"Well," said the man. "I'll just try and do that. I guess you're right—I suppose I could find someone who's got it worse than me, huh?"

"Buddy," I said, smiling patiently. "You still haven't got it right. You probably couldn't find anybody who's got it any better."

It's true. Even the people who have got it rough in America have it significantly better than the majority of the world. To say that you could "probably find someone who's got it worse" is no different than saying "I've got it bad." How often do you ask someone how they're doing, and they respond with something like, "not too bad"? That is another one of my pet peeves. Not too bad? Is that the best we can do? What a dumb message! That means they've got it bad, just not TOO bad.

When someone asks you how you're doing, you need to have something good prepared to say every single time. It shouldn't be difficult to do.

God Has Blessed America

On one occasion, I was speaking to a room of about 14,000 people with the Kiwanis Club. To put it simply, Kiwanis is an organization that gets together, decides what a community needs, raises the money, and gets it done. People typically join Kiwanis for two reasons: either to help others, or help themselves. The ones who join to help themselves usually end up quitting if they don't have a heart change early on, but every once in a while we get to see their motivations change, and they start doing stuff for the right reasons.

In this particular instance, we had just finished saying the pledge of allegiance, and it was my turn to speak. I approached the microphone and asked the crowd, "Now we just pledged to the flag of the greatest country in the world. Do you all think this is the greatest country in the world?"

The crowd roared in agreement, as they normally do when I ask this question.

I went on. "How many of you were in the top five percent in your class?"

About five percent of the crowd raised their hand. "Now that's pretty good, isn't it? If I had been in the top five percent of my class, my mother would have passed out from pure joy. I was lucky to be in the top half."

The crowd chuckled.

"Now guess what percent of the world lives in the United States? I've given you a hint—it's about five percent. We're in the top five percent of the world, just by living in America. But if you add to that having a job, a car, a house, a healthy body, and so many other blessings, then I would guess we're in about the top one twentieth of one percent of the world. Let me tell you something: if you make over $37,000 a year, you're in the top one percent of the world.

"What's that song we all sing so often? 'God Bless America'? Well if you ask me, we should be singing 'God Has Blessed America'! So why has God blessed us this way? How come we weren't born in Somalia, or Syria, or any other poor country in the world?"

The room was quiet for a moment. I continued.

"He blessed us," I continued, "so that we can be a blessing to others. That's the only reason!"

I believe that God created us to be a blessing to others.

So why are we so ungrateful? Why is it that when you ask someone how they're doing, they almost always respond with the classic "okay"? To me, "okay" means average. But when we look at the rest of the world, we Americans don't even know the meaning of average.

The "average" person lives in one room, with a dirt floor, two chairs, a table, and sometimes a bed. Americans have never seen average. We're so far above it that we've never even come close to it. We've never seen true hunger. We can get in our cars and drive from the Atlantic Ocean to the Pacific Ocean without worrying about being shot at, and stop 500 different places to get clean sheets and a good meal. Yet, even here in America,

I hear people complaining all the time. Do you ever wonder if God looks down and thinks, "What else can I do for those ungrateful Americans?" Do you know some people who you think will probably die whining? Don't be one of them!

Just Alike, But Totally Different

I think the person who taught me the most about how blessed we are was a friend of mine named Billy Bob Holiday. Billy Bob was disabled as a result of cerebral palsy. He couldn't walk, couldn't talk, and could barely feed himself. When I was the chairman of United Way, we made a film about Billy Bob for a fundraiser. For those who are unfamiliar with United Way, it is an organization that raises lots of money each year, and then distributes it to agencies that help people. They typically get the whole community involved, and each year they select a chairman—that happened to be me in this particular year.

One day, I went to pick up Billy Bob at his house. My 10-year-old son's bicycle was in the back of my pickup truck at the time. When I got to Billy Bob's house I had to put his wheelchair into the back of my truck, where the bicycle was. As I was doing this, I noticed that the wheels on the bicycle were exactly the same kind as the wheels on Billy Bob's wheelchair.

I looked at the two sets of identical wheels and thought about how blessed my boy was to be riding a bicycle instead of in a wheelchair. The image stuck with me so much that we made Billy Bob the focus of our fundraiser video.

It just seemed so strange to me that we could sit there and complain about petty, unimportant things, when my friend Billy Bob had been that way his entire life and would never see any improvement. What a difference there was in those two sets of wheels. My son was born able to ride a bicycle, and used those wheels for fun and enjoyment. Billy Bob was born with cerebral palsy and had no choice but to use those wheels just to make it through the day.

Just a few years before, we had given Billy Bob his first wheelchair. He was very poor and had never owned onc before.

This wheelchair had air tires, which was a big deal at the time. When we gave it to him, I saw a little tear in his eye. He was so grateful to finally have his own wheelchair.

Billy Bob had so much to teach me about joy. One day, I was

pushing Billy Bob in his wheelchair very fast in my backyard, as he loved to do. Suddenly, one of the wheels hit something, and the chair stopped. It's pretty easy to stop a man who weighs seventy-five pounds, but pretty hard to stop a man who weighs ten pounds less than a quarter of a ton. I lurched forward involuntarily and knocked Billy Bob right out of his chair.

The wheelchair went tumbling away, and I couldn't help but keep moving, falling right over Billy Bob. I got up, brushed myself off, and rushed over to Billy Bob to check on him. I was startled to hear him making the worst noise I had ever heard.

"Billy Bob! Are you okay?" I shouted as I stood over him.

And then I realized with relief, that the noise Billy Bob was making was laughter. He was laughing harder than I had ever heard him laugh. What I had thought to be a crisis had been the most fun Billy Bob had ever had. From that point on, any time I was with Billy Bob, he would always make a

certain gesture, which I knew meant that he wanted me to tell the story of the time he had a wreck in his wheelchair in my backyard. I can't count the number of people I told that story to. It was truly one of the highlights of Billy Bob's life.

My wife and I used to put on a party for disabled individuals every month. We would take them on field trips and show them a good time, and give their parents a break and a chance to do something else. We would sing with them, play with them, and they would have the time of their lives. Seeing the joy that these people had in such difficult circumstances was one of the reasons I wanted to be involved with United Way in the first place.

When I first started working with United Way, I had to cold call people asking for money. Well, I did a pretty decent job, I guess, and next thing I knew they wanted me to be the chairman. I quickly learned that this was the best job in Knoxville, because it gave me the opportunity to learn who the givers were. While some people give reluctantly, others realize that giving is a true blessing. I have learned that being on the giving end of charity is one of the greatest blessings God has given me. Helping others is not a duty or an obligation; it's the most unbelievable privilege that has ever existed.

When I was fundraising for United Way, a lot of people would tell me, "I'll join your board, but I'm not going to raise money." And I understand where they were coming from.

Raising money is hard work! But if something is hard and you don't want to do it, it's probably the right thing to do—a rule of thumb for life. I believe that if you adjust your mindset, you will see that it's not hard— it just takes guts.

You can't ask people for money if you're not giving yourself. Any time someone calls me on the phone asking for money for some cause, I always ask them, "Are you getting paid to do this?" And if they say they are, I say, "Well, I don't give to people who are getting paid to raise money, because I don't know where your heart is." But if they say they are a volunteer, that makes a whole lot of a difference to me. A lot of people do it because they really love to help people, and those are the people I want to give to. It really is more blessed to give than to receive.

Changing Negatives to Positives

We have so much to give, and we take it all for granted.

Another man I got to know through my work with people with disabilities was named Edward. Like Billy Bob, Edward had cerebral palsy, but not as severe. Edward was in a wheelchair, but still able to talk and feed himself.

I would pick up Edward from a crummy old run-down house where about ten disabled people lived. Every time I went over there, I walked in to the same sight: about five or six people with disabilities gathered around an old black and white television. It was quite a sad environment to be in.

I would pick up Edward from this house to take him to our event, and I would roll him in his chair out to my car. I had to pick him up and put him in the car, but before I did, I had to take a deep breath. As you can probably guess, this was because when you are confined to a wheelchair, you don't get to clean yourself very often, resulting in a lingering stench.

Eventually, Edward got to move to a new home that was for people who had some ability to take care of themselves, but still needed some help. The first time I visited Edward in his new home, and I saw a look of excitement I had never seen on him.

"Bo, guess what?" said Edward.

"What?" I said.

"There's someone who here who helps me take a bath every day!" he said happily.

As he said this, I noticed that he had a tear in his eye.

Again, I thought about how blessed I am to get to bathe every day without even having to think about it, and it gave Edward so much joy to partake in this privilege I had never thought twice about.

There were so many experiences like this one in my time working with United Way that made me realize just how good we have it. On another occasion, I was visiting a place called Great Start, which is a United Way agency that focuses on ensuring that young children are born healthy and have the care they need to develop and mature until they are old enough to go to school. I got to hold in my arms a four-week-old baby that was born addicted to crack cocaine.

As I looked at the helpless child, I started thinking about the two sets of tires in the back of my truck. I thought about Billy Bob's laughter after having a wheelchair wreck in my backyard. I thought about Edward's excitement over getting to take a bath. And I looked at this baby that was born addicted to drugs, due to circumstances beyond its control.

At that moment, I told myself, Bo Shafer, you are going to stop complaining right now.

That was in 1983, and I haven't complained since.

I have committed to coming up with a positive to balance out any negative that someone presents me with. I'm getting pretty good at it.

"Oh, it's raining again, I'm so tired of rain!" Well, if it wasn't raining we'd be living in a desert.

"Doggone it, my car broke down!" Well, thank the Lord you've got a car. How many do you have? Two? Wow, what a blessing!

"My hot water heater is broken!" Do you know how blessed you are to have water in your house, let alone hot water?

There is a hardware store that I go to frequently, and one of the ladies that works there always greets me with a smile when I walk in. One day, I walked in and was surprised to see that she had a frown on her face.

"What are you frowning for?" I asked her.

"Well, I just got back from vacation and had a horrible time," said the woman.

"Vacations are supposed to be fun!" I objected.

"I know it, but you're never going to believe this—I got bitten on the cheek by a spider."

For a moment, I was stumped. I was going to have to think hard about this one. After a moment, here's what I came up with.

"Well you know what," I said, "I bet that spider is still smiling. I bet that's the sweetest bite he's had in six months! If I was a spider and I saw you coming, I'd jump right on your cheek and do the same thing! How could he resist?"

I thought her face was going to crack open she was smiling so big.

Now of course, these are small things; not every negative situation is easy to come up with a positive. But I think if you dig deep enough, there's always something there.

My wife passed on from cancer in 2009. We were married for 43 years. I can't count how many times people have told me, "I'm so sorry you lost your wife."

With a smile on my face, I always reply, "When you lose something, you don't know where it is. I know exactly where she is."

My wife is in Heaven, and even if she could come back, she wouldn't do it for two reasons. First, because she loves where she is. Second, because she knows we will all be there together someday.

I don't even use the word "die" anymore. I prefer to say "changed locations". This is just one way you can change your outlook on the things that cause us pain in life.

Are you a thermostat or a thermometer? Do you adapt to the environment around you, or do you change the environment around you? You have the power to change your surroundings with your attitude. Are you humbly grateful, or are you grumbly hateful?

It's easier than you think it is to make someone smile.

Some people hand out a business card when they meet someone for the first time; I hand out a piece of bubblegum. It's such an easy way to brighten someone's day, and after you hand someone a piece of bubble gum when they're expecting a business card, they never forget you. The first time I give them one, it catches them off guard. The next time I see them, I can always see the hope in their eyes as they wonder if I've got any gum with me. At a certain point later, they will just hold out their hand expectantly. One time

I handed a man a piece of bubblegum, and a nearby grown man looked at me expectantly with his hands on his hips and said, "Where's mine?"

I give out about 300 pieces of bubble gum every week, and I estimate I've given out more than a million pieces of in my lifetime, and it never fails to produce a smile. That adds up to 999,999 smiles, if you take one away for the one man who got mad at me for tossing him a piece of bubble gum instead of handing it to him. I don't remember all the smiles, but I certainly remember the one grump who responded with a frown.

If you remember how blessed you are and concentrate on changing every negative in your life into a positive, you will change everyone around you, as well as yourself.

Problems Aren't Problems—They're Lessons

I don't use the word "problems". I prefer to use the word "lessons".

People love to complain about their problems, but normally they can't even remember what they were complaining about a month later. Everyone has problems. They are a part of life! There is one community in every town that never makes any mistakes or has any problems. It's called a cemetery.

The Apostle Paul tells us in Romans 5:2 that problems are good for us: "We can rejoice, too, when we run into problems and trials, for we know that they are good for us—they help us learn to be patient. (TLB)"

When you were four years old, what did you worry about? Nothing! Why? Because you knew that your parents were going to take care of you. You didn't have to worry about what to eat, what to wear, anything! Now, does that mean your parents weren't tough on you? Did it mean that they never disciplined you? Of course not. But whatever they did was in your best interest, because they loved you.

Similarly, we have a Heavenly Father who loves us and has promised to take care of us. Does that mean that he is going to make sure our life is easy? Not at all. Hebrews 12:6 says, "For the LORD disciplines those he loves, and he punishes each one he accepts as his child (NLT)." That sounds like a parent, doesn't it?

We all know children who have never known discipline. You can tell because they are spoiled rotten. God disciplines us because we are His children; it is how we know that He loves us. So we can take comfort in this whenever we encounter problems of any kind.

For most of our problems, we should be thankful that they are so minor. Have you ever heard someone who has a cold complain about being sick? Let's think about that for a moment. What if God told you, "Okay, well, everybody gets sick now and again, and it looks like it's your turn. Now, I'm going to make you sick, but I'm going to bless you and let you choose what kind of sickness you get." What would we all pick? A cold! There are so many awful diseases, so if you ever get a cold you ought to get on your knees and say, "Thank you, Lord, for just giving me a cold!"

One time I ran into a lawyer who looked worn out, and told me he had had a horrible morning.

"A horrible morning?" I said. "A horrible morning for a lawyer would be one where the phone never rings, no one comes to see you, you have nothing to do, and you don't get to bill any hours. Now, was this morning a horrible morning, or was it an extremely busy morning?"

This man had "too much" to do. But having too much to do is the finest thing that can happen to anybody. If you've got a job and you don't have anything to do, you'll get fired!

A similar story happened to me once when I was at a convenience store. A woman had about seven or eight people in line at the cash register, and I heard her complain about how "stressful" her day was.

Now, the word "stressful" is sort of a pet peeve of mine.

We as Americans don't know what real stress is.

"Ma'am," I said to her. "If you'll give me about ten minutes, I bet I can easily find ten people who would just love to have your job. Would you like me to go hunt them down?"

"No," she said sheepishly. "I guess not."

Never complain about being busy. Busyness is a blessing!

Blessed are the flexible, for they shall not be bent out of shape.

A Brother Like That

I heard a story once about a man who had just been given a brand new car by his brother. This man went to one of his friends and started bragging to him about what his brother had done.

"You are not going to believe this, but my brother just bought me a brand new car," the man proudly said to his friend. "Boy, I bet you wish you had a brother like that," he said.

"No sir," said the man's friend. "I wish I could be a brother like that."

Instead of being envious of his friend's new car, this man only wished he could be able to bless someone else in the same way. That's the kind of person we should all strive to be. God puts people in front of us every day that we can be a blessing to; we just have to be looking for them. And when we find them, don't make excuses…do something about it.

Don't get me wrong, I'm not saying you have to do something as extravagant as buying a person a car to be a blessing to them. Something like a simple act of kindness or words of encouragement can make someone's day. Simple things like:

Telling the lady behind the register at the grocery, "You have the nicest smile."

When you pass someone sweeping the floor at the big box store say, "It looks really nice. You're doing a good job."

If you happen to be outside when the trash truck stops at your house saying "Thanks, guys. We appreciate what you do for us."

Remember we have the chance to spread blessings everywhere we are.

"Stuff"

Do we really have it made? Let's take a look at the houses we live in.

After my many travels with Kiwanis and especially after a recent trip to Indonesia I have concluded that by far the majority of us don't live in houses we live in palaces. Let's talk about how we live.

How many of us have a room in our house that we haven't ventured into in a week?

How many of us have more potties in our house than we have potters?

How many of us have several sets of fine china, silverware, and a top of the line dishwasher but the last time we had company we used paper plates?

How many of us have drawers (not the kind you wear) in our house that we can only open half way…we have to reach in a pat down all that "stuff".

If a burglar broke into our house and we needed to hide under the bed…. couldn't do it…too much "stuff" under there.

How many of us have hopped into the car (that's the one not blocked by the other2) and headed to the mall just to see if there is "something" we might want to buy?

Then once we buy that "something" we get back in the car and our first thought is "where am I going to put it?" Too much "stuff."

How many of us have to park our cars in the drive way because our garage is full of "stuff?"

How many of us have three closets crammed full of nothing to wear?

When we do get something new we have to pry the hangers apart to find a space for it. The advantage is that the new garment is automatically pressed!

Too bad we are not centipedes … that way we could wear all those shoes in our closet (my wife says I'm getting a little personal here!) More "stuff"

The point I'm making here is we have never had a need (food, clothing, and shelter) but we are covered up in "wants" resulting in:

Stuff … Stuff … Stuff!

Let's us know … We've Got It Made

Life Lessons

Starting Life Well

I always like to tell young people that you don't learn how to do your job while you're in school. You learn it while you're on the job. There is no better teacher than experience. For most people, their first job is a wakeup call, and causes them to have to grow up quickly. But this is a time in your life when you can start developing good habits to help prepare you for your life down the road.

Many young people like to complain that the things they are learning in school will not be relevant to them in the long run. One time, I was speaking to a group of students, and attempted to explain to them why they needed to be educated.

"How many of you have ever broken an arm?" I asked. A few students raised their hand.

"What does the doctor do for you when you break your arm?"

"He puts a cast on it," one student said.

"Yes," I said. "And why does he put a cast on it?" "So it will heal right," said another student.

"Exactly," I told them. "He has to make sure your arm is immobile so that you can't move it around while it's healing. And what does your arm look like when you take that cast off?"

Another student offered, "It's weak."

"It sure is. It's weak and useless, because you haven't been using those muscles. When you are not using your muscles, they become weak. Does the hardest work you ever do consist of pushing buttons with your thumb? Do your thumbs get more exercise than any other part of your body? If your thumbs are the muscle you use the most, you'd better seriously think about that.

"When we lift weights to make our muscles stronger, we are making our muscles do what they don't want to do, aren't we? Our muscles want to relax. But when we make them do what they don't want to do, they grow stronger. Now, there's another part of your body that's exactly the same way. Your brain. Now, how many of you like to do homework?"

Several students groaned.

"When you do homework," I continued. "You are making your brain do what it doesn't want to do. Just like your muscles, you are making it stronger. When you go to school and study, your brain grows. It becomes stronger. You start thinking differently. That's why you go to school. It's so that you can learn how to think. I went to school myself when I was your age, and I had to learn how to do square roots. Well, I work in the insurance business now, and I can assure you I've never had to take the square root of an insurance policy. But I had to learn square roots anyway. You don't learn your job at school, you learn how to think at school."

There is plenty that you can learn in college just from being on your own for the first time. When you are in your dorm room and you throw your socks on the floor, you learn that your socks aren't going to just hop up and throw themselves into the washing machine. Your mother isn't there to do your laundry for you, and she's not there to tell you to study either. Going away to school teaches you self-discipline.

Once you get out of school and join the workforce, you need to start saving regularly for retirement. I started putting money in the bank when I was twenty-two years old, thanks to my father's urging. Without his wisdom, I probably would have never thought about it at that age. By the time I was sixty-five, I was amazed at how much I had saved.

Whenever I ask a young person if they have started saving money yet, they will frequently respond with, "I'm trying." You're trying? More often than not, that means you're not! Saving up money for the future is terribly important, and you've got to start early. There is always a way that you can save money, and it always means making a sacrifice. There is never any reason you should buy a brand new car, unless you've got the money to pay cash for it. Buy a used one!

One man told me he was "trying" to save money. He was probably forty years old already, and had three children.

"Let me ask you a question," I said to this man. "Do you have one of those great big televisions?"

"Yes," he said. "I've got three of them."

So, what was this man doing? He was letting his feelings control his financial state, instead of his reason.

Whenever I see young people working in food service, I often ask them if they are going to school. Many of them say that they are, and I always encourage them and tell them they are doing the right thing. Whenever I encounter someone who says they're not in school, I ask them why. They normally say that they can't afford it. That's when I say, "You're buying a car, aren't you?" You could go to school if you want to. You don't have to save up to buy some fancy car. Just save up $2,000 and get a little old car that's just good enough to get you where you need to go.

The same goes for buying your first house. You can tell a lot about what a man thinks about himself by the size of his house. Buy a tiny little house for your first house. You don't need a big house until you have children, and you normally can't afford one until then anyway. Many families don't end up moving into a bigger house until their children are older, and by that point they are about to be heading to college soon. Then they are left alone with their spouse in a big empty house. If you can manage to stay in a small house even with kids, you are better off. If you're decent with tools, save some money by buying yourself a fixer-upper.

These are just a few of the ways that you can start being responsible early in life to prepare for the future. If you put these ideas into action, I assure you it will pay off in the long run.

Honor Your Father and Mother

When I first moved out of the house, I had no idea that my mother ever thought of me again. But once I got to be a parent myself, I realized that a child is never far from their parent's mind. You have no idea how much your parents love you, and you can't know until you become a parent yourself.

Whether you are a child or a full grown adult, you need to make sure that you always pay attention to your mother. Mothers are the most special people in the world. They care about you. They worry about you. And sometimes they may get on your nerves, but it's only because of how much they love you.

I once asked a group of about twenty-five teenage girls how many of them got mad at their mother for always wanting to know where they were going and when they were coming home. More than half of them raised their hands.

"Suppose you were driving through the woods, ran your car off the road, hit a tree and were hurt really bad," I said to them. "And there was no one that came looking for you. You would feel pretty bad if that happened, wouldn't you? So when your mother seems overbearing or protective, keep in mind that it is really a blessing to be so loved by someone."

I was in an office one time where three women worked. I did not know these women, but I often strike up conversations with people I don't know. I said to them, "These boys don't pay enough attention to their mothers, do they?"

Being typical mothers, they immediately began making excuses for their sons, but one woman looked at me with a very serious expression and said, "They sure don't."

I told this to some men recently, and as I recounted the story I could see the hurt in their eyes. They were realizing that they had done the same thing to their own mothers. It's so easy to forget to give our mothers the attention they deserve. Even as you get older, it's easy to forget that our mothers keep loving us even as we grow up. When God told the Israelites through the Ten Commandments to honor their mothers and fathers, he was not just talking to the children. He was talking to the adults. If you are blessed to have parents still living, make sure they know how much you appreciate them.

When I walked into my office on my birthday recently, I was surprised to find a picture of the Panama Canal sitting on my desk. It was my son who had put it there, so I asked him why he had done it. He told me that he had planned a trip for the two of us, and that we were going to go through the Panama Canal. We travelled one day, spent two days there, and returned. I have shared this with so many people, because it meant so much that my son had made a special effort to spend time with me. I never thought about doing something like that when I was his age, but he did.

I encourage you to do the same for your parents. When they get to be about sixty years old, plan a trip for you and them. And if your children see you treating your parents this way, they are likely to give you the same treatment.

My father passed on at the young age of 59 leaving my mother a widow. Sometime later I asked her if she planned to do any "courting." In her typical straight forward manner her response was: "Let me tell you something, son, growing old with a man is one thing, but marrying an old man is something else and I'm not interested in that."

One day when she was in her early 70s I called her up to say "hello". As the conversation wound down she began thanking me so profusely for calling. After hanging up her "thank you" weighed heavy on me and I finally said to myself 'Bo Shafer, you are not paying enough attention to your Mama.' I called her right back and said "Mama, put me down for lunch every Wednesday for the rest of your life." That started a tradition that lasted about 30 years (Mama passed at 104!). Years later she joked that if I had known how long she would live I wouldn't have made that promise but those weekly lunches meant so much to each of us.

Lots of Mama's friends knew about our weekly lunches and when I would see one of them they would almost always make a comment about them.

Unfortunately, my father had passed before I figured out how important special time with your parents is to you and them. Be smarter than I was and don't wait until it too late. Remember, your children are watching you!

Thank God that Work is Hard

I went into the insurance business following in my father's footsteps. I learned quickly that working in insurance is hard work, but when I was growing up I never once heard my father complain about his work.

I've talked to a lot of fathers who say things like, "I would never want my son to be in this business." They go home and complain about their jobs in front of their children, and then their children aren't interested in that work. Well, no wonder! I think this not only keeps children from going into their parents' businesses, but it negatively affects their work ethic going forward.

Work is hard. If it was easy, they'd call it play. Thank God that your work is hard, because if it was easy, they'd be paying someone else $7.50 per hour to do it. People who complain about their jobs being hard don't seem to realize that work is inherently difficult—that's what makes it work. If you ran out of problems to solve at your job, you'd just get fired because there would be no more work to do. The more problems you have in your work, the more thankful you should be! You are hired to solve problems, not to complain about them.

I played football at the University of Tennessee from 1956 to 1958. When I first went out for the team, 127 freshmen came out. I was absolutely petrified. I was surrounded by strong athletic young men, and felt so unqualified compared to them.

At the end of my four years, only 10 of those 127 freshmen were left. They started dropping like flies after the very first practice, quitting the team left and right. Why were they quitting? Well, because it was hard! They weren't willing to put in the hard work they knew it would take to be successful. They probably came from some small town somewhere where they were the best player in their youth league, and they weren't used to actually getting knocked down. They were quitting because they had absolutely no commitment. If you're going to do anything well, you've got to be totally committed. If you're not committed, don't even bother trying to be good at something.

We've Got It Made *by Bo Shafer*

My daddy always told me, "Son, when you start something, don't you stop until you finish it." Boy, that virtue that my father passed on to me sure was tested when I was playing football at UT. Back then, they wouldn't even give us water during practice. Going without water was how you got in shape. You would start sweating, and about forty-five minutes later you didn't have any sweat left. If somebody offered you $10,000 to spit, you couldn't come up with any spit to spit. I used to lose about eleven pounds every single practice. Getting knocked down, beaten up, over and over and over. But quitting never crossed my mind. Why? Well, I was committed.

You've got to be committed if you want to do anything at all. You can be committed to stopping your complaining. You can be committed to having a positive attitude everywhere you go. You can be committed to being a good husband. You can be committed to your job—anything.

I frequently talk to high school students with Key Club, which is a high school level version of Kiwanis. Similar to Kiwanis, every year the club commits to finding projects to do around the school in order to help people.

"You can never accomplish anything unless you hustle," I was telling the students one day. "You have to make good things happen. They don't just happen by themselves."

"How many of you have to cut the grass at home?" A few of the boys raised their hands.

"When you come home from school and the grass needs cutting, what do you do?"

After a short silence, one boy chimed in, "I cut it." "Wrong," I said. "You don't even notice it needs cutting." A few of the other boys snickered.

"Now, two or three days later," I continued, "your daddy says, 'Son, looks like it's time to cut the grass.' Then what do you do?"

"Then I cut it," said the same boy.

"Do you?" I asked. "Or do you come up with some silly excuse for why you can't do it right now?"

I saw by the boy's expression that I had guessed correctly. "It's the first time you've remembered you have homework to do since the last time he asked you to cut the grass. Right?" I asked.

The boys agreed, amused.

"So now your daddy says, 'Son, if you don't cut the grass right now, you're going to be in big trouble.' Now what do you do?"

The boy from before was hesitant this time. "Now I definitely cut it," he said.

"Maybe," I said. "But what kind of job do you do?" "Probably not very good," he said.

"Just enough to get by, huh?" I said. "Well, most people stay in that mode for their whole life. They have to be told exactly what to do, and when to do it. They have to be watched carefully to make sure they do it right. And even when they do, they only do just enough to get by. Now is the time to break those habits. You can't make anything good happen if you're in that mode of thinking. It takes commitment to get things done right."

"Now let's change the situation," I went on. "You're twenty-five years old. You've been married about six months. You've got a good job. You just got a raise. You get off work, you drive home, and lo and behold, the grass needs cutting. What do you do?"

"You cut it," said one of the students.

"Who told you to?"

"Nobody."

"And what kind of job do you do?"

"I do a good job."

"That's right, you do," I said. "Because it's your house, so you've taken ownership of it."

Unfortunately, some people still stay in that first mode of thinking for their whole life. These are the people who complain about their job, their boss, and their co-workers. They come into the office at 7:59 and leave at 5:01. They have to be told exactly what to do at all times, and they have to be constantly supervised to make sure they do it right. They whine and whine, and they never get anywhere. Even when they do get something done, they do just enough to get by. These are not the people that will end up becoming owners, or managers, or presidents. In fact, many of them will be hunting a job after a while.

So how do you make sure you don't become one of these people? You've got to get in the mode of looking for something that needs to be fixed or created. You've got to do it without being told, and do it right without being supervised. If you follow these simple steps, you'll be forming a good habit and you'll create a sound foundation for the rest of your life. This is what I call hustling. It's just making good things happen.

Good things don't happen unless you make them happen. Bad comes up easy, but you've got to make good happen. This refers to every aspect of life. If it's hard and you really don't want to do it, it's probably the right thing to do. Hard work is an opportunity to grow, and we should thank God that we are capable of working hard.

Make Sure Your Habits Are Good

You need to start right now to change your mindset.

Habits are being formed in your life now that won't be broken.

If your door knob is loose, go get a screwdriver and tighten it! Don't sit there and do nothing. Don't yell, "Daddy, the door knob's loose!" Fix it now. If you're in the bathroom and there's no towel, don't just reach over and use the toilet paper to dry your hands… go get a towel! If you see some trash laying on the ground, don't say "Somebody really should pick that up" and then move on… pick it up yourself! Once you get into the mindset of action, it will get easier and easier.

One way to get into this mindset is to start taking initiative in the workplace. When you first get a job, you have to learn what your boss likes. If you have a problem, come up with three possible solutions. Let them pick which one they like best. As time goes on, you'll start to be able to predict which solution your boss will choose, and then you can start to make those decisions for yourself.

I got into a habit early on of getting work done when I saw a need, without having to be told to do it. When I was 14 years old, my father suggested that I purchase my first house to fix up and rent. This was intended as a way for me to make some extra money, but it was also an incredible learning experience. I had to borrow my first $800 to get my first house, but by the time I was in high school, I had about twelve houses—the first one which I rented for $20 a month.

I learned so much through that experience. I learned how to paint, how to install sheetrock, how to fix toilets, and how to fix pipe leaks, and even how to deal with irritable people who are never satisfied. When I was younger, if there was a leak my father would hire a plumber to take care of it—but he would bring me along to watch and learn. Even though my father had a fulltime job, he would often be working on the houses right alongside me.

I learned a lot of hard skills through these experiences, but most importantly, I learned about self-discipline. It certainly wasn't easy. I quickly figured out that as soon as you dealt with one problem, the next one is just around the corner. Something always needed fixing. That may sound discouraging, but the good news is that you can learn to fix or build anything if you're willing to put the time into it. You can learn how to lay tile, how to fix plumbing issues, how to fix a light switch—only if you're willing to put the work in. Many people will say, "Well, I don't know how to do that," and that's the end of it. Instead of asking someone to do something for you, try asking them to teach you how to do it, so that next time the problem comes up you can fix it yourself. You'll be amazed how easy it is to fix something once you've done it yourself just one time.

When I grew up, I followed in my father's footsteps and did the exact same thing with my son Andy. He always had four or five houses that he was working on when he was in high school. He couldn't do it all himself; I spent a lot of Saturdays working alongside him when I would have rather have been at the lake. But I feel so blessed to see all the things he is capable of doing because he put the work in early on in his life.

When we see people that seem to be better off than we are, we tend to envy them. This is a dangerous habit that only leads to bitterness and entitlement. Many people have the incorrect mindset that successful people are crooks. They think that anyone who has a lot of money must have come to it in some unfair way. From my experience, this isn't true at all. The majority of the wealthy people I know are intelligent and hardworking people that learned the principle that good things don't happen unless you make them happen. You can't envy what someone has if you're not willing to make the sacrifices that they made to get where they are.

Even though the houses that I worked on in my teenage years were an enormous benefit to me, I sure had to make some sacrifices in the process. I frequently had to tell my buddies I couldn't hang out with them on the weekend because I had to go paint a house. But the fact that I could pass along the things my father taught me to my own son makes it all worth it. After all, if it's hard and you don't want to do it, it's probably the right thing to do.

Relationships

Communication is Key For Healthy Relationships

Good relationships with other people are one of the greatest gifts God gives us as humans. Throughout your life you will have so many important relationships that have a part in making you the person you are, and it is important not to take any of these relationships for granted. Whether it is a family member, a friend, a child, or a spouse, every important human relationship you have in your life has one thing in common: if you want it to be healthy, you have to nurture it.

One of the things that is key to nurturing a healthy relationship is communication. However, communication consists of much more than just words. According to a scientific study that was done, when you are having a conversation, only 7% of the communication happens through the words that you say. 55% of communications comes across through body language, and 38% comes across through your tone of voice. In today's world, there are so many options for ways to communicate with people. As technology advances, it seems like there are more and more communication mediums. Not only can you call someone on the phone; you can text them. You don't have to write someone a letter anymore; you can email them. And now there are many forms of online social media that provide even more options. While none of these communication mediums are inherently bad, I believe that there is no replacement for a face-to-face conversation. Think about the statistic mentioned above—if you are texting someone, you may be only getting across 7% of the point you are trying to make! With no room for body language or tone of voice, it is very easy to misinterpret someone's intended message over texting. While texting can be a fine way to have a quick conversation, I firmly believe that you cannot build a relationship through texting.

Even if you cannot physically have a conversation in person with someone, it is always better to speak over the phone if possible, instead of relying on written communication. You may not be able to incorporate body language into your conversation, but at least you can incorporate tone of voice— which takes our percentage from 7% up to 45% of the effect of an in-person conversation.

These days it is becoming more and more common for dating relationships to be entirely based on text messages. Texting is so easy that oftentimes a boy will text a girl all day long, but he can't get up the nerve to call her. Girls, if the majority of your communication with a boy you like is only taking place through text messaging, then send him a text telling him to call you. When he calls you, ask him to come and see you in person. Then, you can look him in the eye and have a real conversation with him, and you'll really be able to see what kind of a person he is.

The same thing goes for boys too. Boys, if there is a girl you like and you want to build a relationship with her, don't just text her; call her. When you call her, ask if you can come see her in person. Then you can have an authentic, intentional conversation and really start to get to know each other.

The best way to have a real conversation with someone you'd like to get to know is to only ask questions that cannot be answered with simply "yes" or "no". Asking someone a question like "Do you like to play sports?" may not really take the conversation anywhere. Instead, ask "What do you like to do for fun?" And then, if it's something you have in common, then you've got something to talk about. But a conversation like that is probably not going to happen through texting. The most convenient medium of conversation is usually not the best one.

When you do something nice for someone, they are going to be more appreciative the more effort you put into what you do for them. Just as we said in the last chapter: if it's hard and you don't want to do it, it's probably the right thing to do. This same principle applies to communication: in general, the harder it is to do, the more people appreciate it. An email means more than a text message, and a hand-written letter means so much more than an email.

I once received an email that was sent out to a distribution list of email addresses that was two full pages long. In the body of the email, there were only two words: "Happy Thanksgiving!" That's all it said. Do you think that message meant anything special to anyone who opened it? Of course not! Anyone can write a two-word message and send it out to everyone they know. A personalized handwritten letter, on the other hand, means more than anything, because it's the harder thing to do.

Write a Letter to Your Father

While we're on the subject of writing—I have developed a habit of telling nearly every man that I meet that he needs to write a letter to his father, if he is able to. I think this is one of the most important things I will talk about in this book. The relationship between a father and son is so special, but we as men often have trouble communicating to each other. It is easier and far more effective to tell your father how much he means to you through a written letter than it is to do in person, and a letter is a physical object that he can keep and treasure for the rest of your life. I guarantee you when your father reads the letter there will be tears in his eyes. And you may even get a tear in your eye when you write the letter, but that's okay— if you get a tear in your eye while you talk to your father in person, you will be tempted to cut the conversation short. That is why I recommend you write a letter instead of just calling him on the phone. If you have children, how much would it mean to you to receive a letter from one of your children, telling you how much you mean to them?

About a year ago, one of my good friends called me up and said, "Bo, you told me twenty years ago to write a letter to my dad. Well, I did exactly what you told me to do. I'm calling you today to tell you that he passed away three days ago. As I was going through his lockbox of important documents, you'll never guess what I found." Sure enough, it was the letter that his son had written him all those years ago. That one simple letter had meant so much to this man that he had held on to it for twenty years.

Of course, you can write a letter to your mother as well, and it will mean the world to her. If you do this for any loved one, once they finally pass on you can rest easy knowing it was one of the best things you've ever done. I only like to specifically tell men to write to their fathers because we have so much trouble talking about our emotions with them sometimes. As a general rule, men do not like to talk about their feelings. Our conversations are more like, "I love you, Dad—what's for supper?" It can be a little easier to write your mother a letter, but that does not make it any less important or meaningful. I believe that everyone should do this—both men and women. I can't tell you how many similar stories I have heard from people who have followed my advice on this subject. I ran into one woman sometime after I had shared it with her.

"Did you ever write that letter to your daddy?" I asked her. "I sure did," she said. "And I didn't just send it to him. I took it to him personally and read it out loud. By the end of it, we were both in tears."

Make a habit of writing handwritten notes to all of the important people in your life. I specifically say handwritten because emails do not count. Email is a fine form of communication, but it does not carry as much meaning as a handwritten letter does. You can do this for your friends, your children, your spouse, your parents—anyone who is important to you. I personally have a desk where I always keep paper, a pen, envelopes, and stamps readily available so that I can write a note to anyone at any time. When I tell men to write a letter to their fathers, I always give them one of my business cards and write a short phrase on it "Write that letter!" And I tell them to place it on their desk and leave it there until the letter is written.

When you do this and see how important it is, don't forget to share the idea with your friends. When I share this with people, I will often hand them a fresh envelope with a stamp on it. You can do this too, and it will greatly increase the chance that they will actually take action. Believe me: if you tell someone to do this and they follow through with it, they will thank you.

The "If Only's"

I used to know two brothers who told me that they had not spoken to one another in ten years. They used to get along just fine, until one day they had some silly disagreement and stopped speaking to each other because of it. Both of them were too proud to just leave it in the past and say "Let's be friends—we're brothers, after all."

These two brothers never reconciled, and eventually, one of them passed away suddenly. That remaining brother probably has a lot of regrets; there is probably so much that he wishes he had said to his brother. Life can be unpredictable, and while we don't like to think about it, we never know how long the people who are important to us will be in our lives.

Sometimes we find ourselves thinking, "If only I'd told her how much I loved her," or, "if only I'd written that letter to my father before he died, telling him how much he means to me."

I had the same barber cut my hair for forty-five years. I never had a reason to go to anybody else, because when I left this man's shop I always felt happy. One day, my barber called me on the phone. "Bo," he said. "If you need a haircut, you'd better come by within the next few days. I'm about to go to the hospital because I've got to get a new valve in my heart. The doctor says it's an emergency and I've got to have it done right away."

It sounded serious, and he said that he was going to be in the hospital for quite some time. So I called my son, who also went to this same barber, and suggested that we throw a little going away party for him. But then as I got to thinking, I thought we might not have the time. I started to change my mind, and said maybe we could do something later instead.

"Daddy," said my son. "Don't wait."

So two days later, we did it. We had a gathering at the barbershop with about twenty of his friends and regular customers. We had a wonderful time, with ice cream and cake, and we prayed over him. He was so surprised. It was such a pleasure to be able to give back to this man who had made us so happy over the years.

Sure enough, he never made it out of the hospital. I am so grateful to my son for encouraging us to not put it off. If we had put it off, we never would have had to chance to let our barber know how much his kindness had meant to us. I suspect the same is true for many of the people who attended the party that day.

If there is anyone in your life that you care deeply about, then you need to take the time right now to figure out what your "If only's" would be if they were to pass away tonight.

What are the things that you would regret not having said or done?

Don't put it off for another time—do it today! Here are some instructions for how you can put this into action right away:

Get out a blank sheet of paper.

Divide it vertically into three columns.

In the leftmost column, list the names of the 7-8 most important people in your life.

In the center column, write the phrase "If they died tonight…" next to each name.

At the top of the rightmost column, write "What would my if only's be?" Underneath that, begin listing all the things you need to say to the people you listed in the first column.

Put this somewhere where you will see it on a regular basis, and start working on them right now! When you take care of one of the names on your list, write the date next to it. It is easy to put this off, thinking you'll come back to it later. Don't do it.

The "If Only's" are awful!

It always means so much to receive a letter or a phone call from someone, especially when you are not expecting it. Throughout the year, I keep a list of everyone I know whose spouse has passed on like mine has. At this point, that list is about a full page long, and it grows longer with each passing month. Especially during the holiday season, I go through this list and I call each person, just to let them know that I'm thinking about them. Since I have been through what they're going through, I know that the holidays can be a sad time when a loved one has passed, and the first year is always the toughest. They seem to appreciate hearing that someone is thinking about them and knows the pain they are going through.

Take Action—Make Something Happen

If you see something that needs to be done, take care of it now. The more you put it off, the easier it will be to forget it. This same principle applies to dating relationships as well.

I often hear young, single men say, "I'm waiting on God to send me a girl."

"No sir," I say to them. "Some of the girls that call you aren't always the marrying kind."

Just as I've said in a previous chapter, good things don't happen unless you make them happen. A lot of these girls may have a boyfriend, but they're still just waiting until the right guy comes along. Most of those girls want to go out with you just as bad as you want to ask them out. But it takes guts. You're afraid you're not good enough, you're afraid they've got a boyfriend— you can come up with any number of excuses, just like the young boy in the grass-cutting scenario.

I came up with a surefire way to find out if any girl would like to go out with you. Here is the process:

Ask her what her favorite restaurant is.

Whatever she says is her favorite restaurant, it's yours too.

Say, "I love that place too! But I hate eating by myself. If I ever having a craving to go to lunch there sometime and have no one to go with, would you like for me to give you a call?"

If she is interested, she'll say yes, and buddy, you ask her out right then! If she says, "Well I would, but my husband will kill me," then don't panic—remember, you haven't asked her out. You haven't done anything wrong! If it's with someone you don't know very well, always make the first date lunch. If it doesn't go well, no pressure—just go back to work, and it's over with.

Never turn down a blind date; just make it a lunch date, so there's no pressure. A lunch date is always a safer option for going out with someone you have never met before. When you're at lunch, you can always say, "Well, I've got to get back to work," if these things don't seem to be going well. A dinner date normally feels like a bigger deal, and it's harder to escape if things get awkward. If a lunch date doesn't go well, it's much easier to end it on friendly terms.

Men, don't be afraid to take action if you see a nice attractive lady in public. Walk right up to her and say, "Now, you may think I'm crazy for saying this, but you're a very pretty lady and I'd love the chance to get to know you better." Trust me—she won't smack you. She will not be insulted. At worst, she'll be flattered. At best, she'll go on a date with you!

I know that my approach must work, because my wife likes to tease me by saying that I must have dated every woman in Knoxville at some point. That may be an exaggeration, but there's some truth in it. I was hunting—and hunting is fun!

Once, I was talking to a young woman who told me that she didn't have a boyfriend. I could tell she was unhappy about it.

"Believe me," I told her. "There is a boy very close to here that is looking for a girl just like you. I guarantee it."

Years ago, before my son was married, we were out eating dinner at a restaurant when I pointed out a cute waitress to him. "You ought to ask her out," I said.

"Daddy, I can't," said my son. "She's got a boyfriend."

"Son," I said, "if I had let that stop me, you wouldn't be here."

And that's the truth. When I met my wife of forty-three years, she had a real serious boyfriend. Of course, it must have been more serious to him than it was to her—because it didn't stop her from going out with me when I asked her.

I have even been on some dates where I would pick up a girl at her house at midnight, when her date had just dropped her off. If you ask a girl with a boyfriend on a date like that and she says yes, then you know she has not found the right person. This goes for both men and women—the vast majority of people who are in a dating relationship are dating someone who they know they aren't going to end up marrying. So while it's important to be respectful and not overstep any boundaries, you should also keep in mind that just because someone is dating someone other than you, you don't have to rule them out entirely.

I've never been a woman, but I have been an eighteen- year-old man, so I know how they think. Most of them can't tell the difference between love and lust. I'm not sure if this applies to women as well. Young people have got to get to the point where they can discern between love and lust.

Physical attraction is going to change over time, so if you don't have a genuine love as a foundation, your relationship is not sustainable.

I love to ask young people, "Do your mother and father go into a wild embrace every time they see each other?" They always laugh and say, "Of course not!" That is why I say you cannot have a lasting relationship that is based purely on physical attraction. Girls, watch how your boyfriend's father treats his wife. That is likely how your boyfriend will treat you. Boys, watch how your girlfriend's mother treats her husband.

This is a good way to get a glimpse at the character of someone you are dating, so that you can begin to see if it can be a sustainable relationship.

Human relationships are one of the most important things in life. Our relationships affect our whole lives, as well as the world around us. People do business and associate with people they know and trust. This is why it is so important to put the time and effort into nourishing relationships and keeping them healthy. You don't build a relationship instantly. Just like a building, you have to build it one brick at a time. In the end, it's worth it to have a lasting a relationship.

Marriage

A Good Marriage is a Little Piece of Heaven

A good marriage is a little piece of Heaven. I've been blessed to never have to experience a bad marriage, but I would assume it's more like a little piece of the other place.

I should probably state right up front before I start talking about marriage that this is all going to come from a man's perspective. I can't speak from a woman's perspective, because I've never been one. But I'll tell you one thing—we men are blessed because we get to marry women. Women got the short end of the stick, because they have to marry men.

In the first chapter of Genesis, God says that when a man and woman get married, they become one. If you truly "become one" with someone else, you are going to make sure that your interests, goals, and priorities are lined up with theirs. If that is true, then you will never be trying to "outdo" each other.

Ephesians 5:21 says that husbands and wives are to "submit to one another out of reverence for Christ." So often, our culture likes to treat the Bible's teachings on marriage unfairly and focus on wives submitting to their husbands. You will rarely hear these people bring up this verse, which clearly states that husbands and wives are both to submit to each other. The Bible says that the husband is the head of the wife, just as Christ is the head of the church. Did Christ come to be served by the Church? Not at all—he came to serve the church. So then, we know that husbands are to serve their wives.

In verses 25-28, Paul goes on to say: "For husbands, this means love your wife, just as Christ loved the church. He gave up his life for her to make her holy and clean, washed by the cleansing of God's word. He did this to present her to himself as a glorious Church without a spot or wrinkle or any other blemish. Instead, she will be holy and without fault. In the same way, husbands ought to love their wives as they love their own bodies. For a man who loves his wife actually shows love for himself."

Here is a simple way to sum this up for daily application: husbands, do more for your wife than you think she does for you.

Wives, do more for your husband than you think he does for you. Try your best to out-serve your spouse for your entire life.

In today's world, it's not very popular to say that a wife (or husband) has a responsibility to be submissive, but that is what we find God's word telling us consistently. Here is a helpful definition of submission that I came across in the Life Application Study Bible: "Submission is a key element of

smooth functioning in any business, government, or family. God ordained submission in certain relationships to prevent chaos. It is essential to understand that submission is not surrender, withdrawal, or apathy. It does not mean inferiority, because God created all people in his image and because all have equal value. Submission is mutual commitment and cooperation.

Thus, God calls for submission among equals. He did not make the man superior; he made a way for the man and woman to work together. Jesus Christ, although equal with God the Father, submitted to him to carry out the plan for salvation....

Submission between equals is submission by choice, not by force. We serve God in these relationships by willingly submitting to others in our church, to our spouses, and to our government leaders."

I have been in the insurance business for my entire life, so I have seen firsthand what it looks like for two people to have a power struggle in a business setting. In any situation like this, no matter what the context, it almost always ends in failure.

If you do not have someone designated as a leader, you have chaos. Someone has to have the role of maintaining focus for a group as they work to achieve a goal—this is why every board must have a chairman. Someone has to be the one to make the tough calls when there are disagreements, and the Bible tells that that in a marriage context, that role has been given to the husband. This is not because he is smarter or better in any way! God has called for submission among equals.

A man's goal in his marriage should be to keep his wife smiling 24 hours per day. You've heard the phrase "When mama's not happy, nobody's happy." I like to add to that phrase, "when daddy's not happy, it really doesn't matter." If Mama's grumpy, nothing goes right in the house. If Daddy's grumpy, it usually doesn't affect the atmosphere of the house as much. For that reason, I believe that a smiling wife is the most beautiful thing in the home.

I was once in a store and I saw a husband and wife arguing about the color of a little throw rug they were thinking about purchasing. I walked up to the husband with a smile on my face and said, "Sir, what's prettier: the color of that rug that you're going to wipe your dirty feet on, or the smile on your wife's face?"

If my wife must submit to me, and my main priority is keeping a smile on her face, then the issue of submission is not a problem, but rather a beautiful picture of Christ's relationship to the church. In any relationship among equals, if someone is not designated as the leader, there will be dissension instead of harmony. But if I love my wife the way Christ loves the church,

I will do everything in the world that I possibly can do to make her happy. We cannot, however, do this without the help of the Holy Spirit. Unconditional love is not natural. We are not born with love for others—we are born addicted to ourselves. This is something we must learn, and it takes time and hard work.

Now, I want to be perfectly clear that I am not talking about situations in which a spouse is abusive. This scripture is talking specifically about submitting to a man who has already submitted himself to Christ. If a man is following Christ closely, then his wife will be following Christ in turn by following her husband.

One thing I learned in the army is that when your commander gives you an order, you don't question it. You do exactly what he says. Even in situations where the person he is giving an order to knows better, they are responsible to follow his orders no matter what. If the lieutenant yells "Charge!" and one guy stands there saying "Not me!" then you've got a problem. Someone has to be a leader, and the same is true in a marriage. Submission is voluntary, and it doesn't mean anyone is better than anyone else.

The Ladder of Love

Have you ever witnessed a group of men that were chatting and joking around, and one of the men makes a degrading joke about his wife? I know I have. I have seen men say negative things about their wives for the amusement of their friends many times, and it never ceases to sadden me.

You should never say anything negative about your spouse to someone else—if you are talking about your spouse in public, only say things that will build them up, not tear them down.

It's very easy to talk yourself into things. You can talk yourself into buying a car—based on whatever your predisposition is, you can find reasons to buy the car or reasons to pass on it. This is why we have to be careful with the things we say. The more we say something, the more we start to believe it. If you talk negatively about your husband or wife on a consistent basis, your love for them will start to decrease.

However, as I've said before, you can find something positive in any situation. Men, if you always speak positively about your wife, and end every conversation by saying "and I love that woman now even more than I did when I married her" then your wife is going to hear about that! And when she hears it, she's going to love you more. And when she does, you will love her more. Over the years, your love will grow and grow.

I call this concept the "ladder of love"—I believe that love is like a ladder, which you can choose to go up or down. If you regularly say negative things about your spouse, you will start to believe them. Your spouse will not love you well, just as you are not loving them well, and your love will diminish over the years instead of growing. It's easy to find something negative to say about someone, so this is something we have to actively fight against. You will see this happen if you pay attention. Husbands and wives will stay together only because of their children. When their children leave, and their love has diminished, the marriage doesn't make it. If they only stay in the marriage for their children, they will have nothing to cling to once the children are gone.

Once I was making conversation with a group of men and women that I didn't know. I said to the men in the group, "Now fellas, remember: women do not snore. They purr."

One of the men (whose wife was present with him) quickly came back with "Yeah? Well, my wife purrs like a chainsaw!"

Everyone laughed—except me.

I looked him straight in the eye and said, "Sir, do you think that made your wife feel good?"

He didn't have a response for me.

Situations like that always sadden me, but they are all too common. Even if it seems clear that you are not being serious, you should never make a joke at the expense of your spouse.

Words have power. Once they are spoken, they can't be taken back. You have a choice as to whether you will speak negatively or positively about something, and what you choose can make all the difference in your marriage.

Keys to a Happy Marriage

After fifty years of happy marriage, I've learned a bunch of things that I believe are real keys to a healthy marriage. Here are some of them that I have discovered.

No Nagging

When I first got married, I had a habit of taking my shoes off when I got home and not always remembering to put them where they belong. After a while, my wife kindly asked me to start putting them away when I took them off, but I kept right on doing the same old thing. One day, I was looking for my shoes where I had taken them off, and I couldn't find them. I eventually looked in the closet, and there they were! Instead of nagging me repeatedly about it, my wife had started to just put them away herself. What a sweet, understanding wife.

When you get married, there will be some things that might annoy you about your spouse. They don't say "for better or for worse" for nothing—and when you get married, you are signing up for some "worse". You need to date someone long enough to figure out what their "worses" are (because there will be some,) and decide whether or not you can deal with them. If you can't, the solution is simple: don't get married.

You and your spouse don't need to be trying to change each other. People change naturally over time, but not because their spouse forced it. Don't marry somebody because you think you can live with this person; marry them because you can't live without them. If in doubt, chicken out.

People have a tendency to make a big deal out of the silliest little things. Going through fourteen years of cancer with my late wife made me realize that everything that we worry about is nothing. All the little things throughout our day that put a frown on our face are, more often than not, big fat pieces of nothing. Last week, you probably had several things that put a frown on your face. Today, you probably don't even remember what those things were. As I always say—blessed are the flexible, for they shall not be bent out of shape.

For example, I like to squeeze my toothpaste out from the bottom of the tube. My wife prefers to squeeze from the middle of the tube. I've always felt that my way is correct, because it keeps all of the toothpaste at the top of the tube, ready to come out. Instead of nagging her about this, I've started going into the bathroom every couple of weeks, and squeezing all of the toothpaste to the top of the tube. Every time I do it, I can hear the toothpaste tube saying "Oh thank you, thank you, thank you!" It may be a little extra work, but it's worth it, because nagging is never good, and it is absolutely no fun for anyone.

Never Say "I Told You So!"

When you tell someone "I told you so", there is a subtle hidden message: "I'm smarter than you, because I thought of it first." That's never a good thing to say to your spouse.

It may sound easy to avoid saying a simple four-word phrase, but it's harder than it sounds. You have to admit that sometimes it's one of most fun things to say. You don't have to say it with your words; sometimes you might be saying with your eyes. Avoiding this phrase (as well as the attitude that it usually comes as a result of) is a great way to make your marriage a lot more pleasant.

Keep the Special Things Special (Not Routine)

Men, never go into the bathroom with your wife except to brush your teeth and comb your hair. There will be some special occasions where it's okay to share the shower, but there's no reason to do any of that other stuff while she's around; that's the way hogs live. Keep treating her with the respect she deserves, no matter the situation. Even when you use the toilet, strive to not make any noise. No one wants to hear that! When you've spent years and years with someone you love, simple things like this may seem silly, but it's important to treat your spouse with dignity even in the bathroom.

On a similar note, keep your clothes on when you're walking

around the house. Again, there are special occasions when you and your spouse are not fully clothed, but what is it that makes things special? Something is only special if it is not part of a routine. Make an effort to keep special things special, and routine things routine.

Chipped Teeth (REAL Important for a Happy Marriage!)

You can tell how happy someone's marriage is by how badly their teeth are chipped. Does this sound funny to you?

Take this all too familiar example.

"Honey, remember we've got to go to that party tomorrow night."

"Party? You never told me about any party!"

"I told you yesterday."

"You did not."

Have you ever had a conversation like this with your spouse? Most married couples have them from time to time. As long as your voice never raises, it's a conversation. Once you raise your voice the slightest bit, suddenly it's an argument.

Most arguments are over nothing except "I'm right, and you're wrong." This is a natural reaction to conflict. Most of these situations must be addressed, but the secret to keeping it a conversation instead of an argument is to grit your teeth (but cover it with a smile) and don't raise your voice. Tell your spouse, "Honey, I'm sorry I thought I told you," even if you know full well that you did tell them. If you keep gritting your teeth at times like this, you'll never have an argument, but you'll probably have bad teeth when you get old.

It's not easy to tell your spouse that they're right when you know that you're right, but when it's over absolutely nothing, who cares? My wife and I have never had an argument in our seven years of marriage, but we have to go to the dentist real often.

Love Notes

Men, when you get married, you need to start carrying a stamp with you in your billfold everywhere you go. Whenever you go on a trip, buy a nice card, write a note on it, and mail it to your wife.

Once I was on a trip with some other men, and I gave each of them a stamp so that they could send their wife a card. One of the men looked at me funny and said, "If I sent her that, she'd think I'd done something awful!" It's such a small thing, but it says so much. I have a stack of all the cards my wife sent me at the office over the years. When you're away from your spouse, a simple note to let them know that you're thinking about them can go a long way.

The Ladder of Love

I have already mentioned the Ladder of Love, but it is worth bringing up again because it is so crucial to having a happy marriage. You should never say anything negative about your spouse to anyone—not even your best friend. Once you verbalize a negative about someone you love, that thought begins to solidify in your mind, and you can talk yourself into not loving them. Remember, a relationship is like a ladder that you can choose to go up or down, and saying negative things about the other person is a surefire way to go down it.

Whenever I talk about my deceased wife and current wife to anyone, I always say, "I'm a blessed man; I've been married to two angels." Word gets around, and that's a much better thing for her to hear than anything negative I might say.

Always Open the Door for Your Wife

Many people will open the car door for their girlfriend or wife early in the relationship, but often they will stop doing this later in life. I always open the door for my wife. It's just another one of those small things that can go a long way in showing your wife that you care. Maybe someone else will see you opening the door for your wife, and decide to do the same for theirs.

Husbands: Compliment Your Wife Frequently

If you go to a party or anywhere with a lot of people, look around and whisper in your wife's ear, "I've checked everybody out, and you're the prettiest one here." When your wife cooks dinner for you, tell her it was the best supper you've ever had. Little compliments like this add up over time and mean a lot to your wife.

One Brick at a Time

The only way to build a building from bricks is to lay one brick on top of another, and repeat that process for a period of time. It might feel tedious, but keep it up and you've got a building in no time. Building a loving relationship is the same way. It just takes loving commitment. Because of our selfish nature, being kind to your spouse at all times is sometimes difficult. However, if you focus on being kind one moment at a time, you will end up with a strong, loving, relationship.

Husbands: Never say "Mom does it this way"

When you're in the kitchen with your wife, you should never say anything akin to "That's not the way my mom does it." In fact, if your wife is in the kitchen, you probably ought to just stay out. This, of course, doesn't just apply to the kitchen, it applies to your life in general. No one wants to be told what to do, and you should just assume she knows what she's doing. It's not worth starting an argument over.

Husbands: The Best Thing You Can Do for your Children is Love their Mother

Your children are paying attention to the way you treat your wife. You can tell them whatever you want, but the best way to teach them what love looks like is to demonstrate it. Not only will this help them by showing them what a godly marriage looks like, but it will affect the way they interact with people on a daily basis.

Hold Hands

Husbands and wives, you should hold hands everywhere you go, whenever possible. It may seem like a simple gesture, but it is a great way to show affection when you are out in public. There is nothing sweeter than seeing an old gray- headed married couple holding hands walking through a parking lot. In a world that is growing more and more cynical toward marriage, this can be a nice reminder that love and marriage really can endure for a lifetime.

Pray Before Every Meal

A husband and wife should make a habit of praying together, and one of the best places to do this is in a restaurant before you eat. Of course, you are not doing it to put on a show for the people around you, but this is another simple way to send the message that you have Christ at the center of your marriage. Any time I am out and see someone else praying before their meal, I always nudge my wife and say, "Look, there's someone else that does it too!"

Praying before meals should be a priority, no matter where you are or who you're eating with. Some people may think you're crazy for initiating a prayer, but some others will be thrilled to find that they're eating with someone with similar values to their own. You'll be surprised to find how many people there are who love Jesus if you just start paying attention.

I was making a phone call once and I dialed the wrong number. I quickly realized this and informed the woman who had answered the phone, who responded by saying, "Well, that's all right. Are you all right with Jesus?" I had no idea who this woman was, but when she said that, I knew that we had something in common. The next thing I knew; we were having a five-minute conversation about how good Jesus is.

Think of the message you are sending when someone sees you and your spouse praying over your meal before you dig in. We pray before we eat so that we can thank God for our blessings as we partake in them, and we should make a habit of this especially when we are out in public.

Say "I Love You", NOT "Love You"

How many times have you ended a conversation with a loved one by thoughtlessly throwing out that short phrase "love you"? It may be a nice sentiment, but it's so quick and easy that we often say it without thinking about what we're really saying. I think that if you truly love someone, you should take the time to say the whole phrase: "I love you." It forces you to slow down a bit and think about what you are actually saying, and it sounds a whole lot more meaningful to the person you are talking to. When you are talking to your husband or wife, take the time to say "I love you." Adding that extra word at the beginning makes the phrase carry a lot more weight.

Husbands: Pay Attention to Opportunities for Compliments

Men, your wife works hard to keep the house looking as good as it does, so pay attention to it and talk about how great it looks. Keeping the house in order takes a lot more work than most men realize, and sometimes this hard work goes unnoticed. When you open the drawer to find a neatly-folded pile of clean clothes, say "Boy, it sure is nice to have a drawer full of clean clothes!" Pointing out the specifics of what your wife has done with the house is a great way to show that you appreciate her.

Similarly, you should always make a point to remember when your wife is getting her hair done. As men, we sometimes tend to notice these things less than women do, so it means so much when you make a point to comment on how great her hair looks. When she tells you she has a hair appointment, write down the date and remember it. Don't trust yourself to notice it when she comes home. Set a reminder on your phone, and then tell her how good it looks! It doesn't have to be dishonest—you're bound to notice it if you're looking for it, but sometimes we as men need that extra reminder.

Consistent Surprises

Men—every once in a while, send your wife flowers for no reason. It's great to send your wife flowers on special occasions, but it means even more if there is no occasion other than that you were thinking about her. This is something that is easy to do and can go a long way in showing how much you care. Everyone loves surprises whether they are big or small; so whether it's a surprise card or flowers, or a surprise trip to your spouse's favorite vacation destination, make sure and plan plenty of surprises within your marriage.

Remember Birthdays and Anniversaries

Husbands, always remember anniversaries and birthdays.

Wives, help your husband out in remembering these things! I've heard many women complaining that their husband never remembers their anniversary, and I always make a point to tell them to remind him when the anniversary is coming up! If you know he is going to forget, don't wait on him to remember it. Tell him! People make honest mistakes sometimes, and men tend to have more trouble remembering occasions like that.

There is no reason to have your feelings hurt over an honest mistake, so if you help each other out everyone will be happier in the end.

Schedule Time to Spend Alone With Your Spouse

I believe that every married couple should strive to have a spontaneous date-night (or better yet an overnight trip) at least three to four times every year. By making this a priority, you can ensure that you can spend some quality, unhurried, undistracted time together on a regular basis. You can plan the whole thing ahead of time and surprise your spouse by taking care of the details before they even know you're planning anything. This gets harder when you have children, but that's when it's the most important. If you don't have grandparents in town that can take care of the kids, then find another couple with children that you can swap out babysitting times with, so that they can do the same thing, too.

Even on a daily basis, you should try to have a few minutes of quality time with your spouse each day. Take some time to ask them how their day was, and then truly listen to them when they tell you. Sometimes the question "How was your day?" can become nothing but a routine, but if you love someone you should want to know about what's going on in their life. This doesn't happen on its own; you've got to make it happen by placing it into your schedule.

Be a United Front When It Comes to Discipline

Your kids are smart. Often times, they will try to "work the system" when they know that Mom and Dad may respond to certain requests differently ("Well, Mom said I could do it!"). It's very important that your children always see you and your spouse as a united front when it comes to discipline. You and your spouse need to know ahead of time how you are going to respond to basic issues that come up with all kids. If something unexpected comes up, then you should respond with something like, "Go get your mother and let's talk about it." Stand firm and support one another's decisions so that you can set a godly example of what it looks like to have a relationship as one.

If Your Spouse Died Tonight, What Would Your "If Only" Be?

Life is short, and you never know just how long the people you love are going to be in your life. As much as we don't like to think about this, our spouses are no exception. I believe that when anyone gets married, they should make a list of the things that they would regret having not done if their spouse were to die that night. Don't just make a list in your head; write it down. That way, you can come back to it and use it as a guide for how you treat your spouse. Work through the list and do each and everything on it, so that you can live knowing you would have no regrets if something were to happen to them.

Make God the Center of Your Marriage

Never be afraid to bring up the name of Jesus in your

conversations with your spouse. If God is the foundation of your marriage, He should be a regular topic of conversation.

Lift up your spouse to the Lord in prayer each day. Study the Bible and pray with your spouse daily.

None of the things listed above will have any lasting impact on your marriage if you do not have God at the center of your relationship. Unconditional love is not normal. We are not born with the ability to

love unconditionally; we are reborn with this ability. As you and your spouse grow together in your love for Jesus, you will grow closer to one another as well.

Parenting

A Benevolent Dictatorship

I'm going to tell you a little story, and keep in mind: this is not biblical. Rather, it is what I've decided to call "Bo-blical".

God made man in the evening. You know how I know that?

Because based on the final product, he must have been tired when he made Adam. I suppose he looked him over, and then thought, "Ugh, I think I can do better than that." So he decided that he would go to bed, get a good night's rest, and then the next morning give it another shot. So he did just that. The next morning, he woke up refreshed, went over to Adam, and took one of his ribs. Do you know what he made with that rib? He made mothers. And that has to be where the term "prime rib" comes from.

Mothers are the most special people in the world. There are no words sweet enough to describe the maternal instinct that they have. They have the hardest and the most important job in the world. Now, daddies are terribly important as well! But there is nothing more special than a mother. They care about you, they worry about you, they tell you to be careful every time you walk out the door. If you think that ends once their children are grown up, you're wrong. It continues forever.

When it comes to raising a family, I believe the four most important jobs are:

- Being a Mother
- Setting the Moral Standard
- Being the Glue that Holds the Family Together
- Making a Living

Between the mother and the father, these four jobs all must be fulfilled in order to have a healthy household.

Obviously, God gave the first job to women—and this one, in my opinion is the most difficult. As I said before, daddies are terribly important, but being a mother is a truly special responsibility, as well as an incredible privilege.

The next job, setting the moral standard, also goes to women. Men are generally incapable of fulfilling this role, especially when they're young. There are exceptions to this, of course, but generally speaking, it is simply an unfortunate truth that men tend to be less steadfast in their morals than women. An eighteen-year-old boy is not likely to say "no" to an eighteen-year-old girl. This job does not necessarily have to do with parenthood, since a man is equally responsible for setting the moral standard in his household, but in a relationship scenario, it seems that the job of setting the moral standard goes to women.

The third most important job in the world is being the glue that holds the family together. And guess what? That one goes to women again! You've probably heard the saying, "When Mama's happy, everybody's happy. When Mama's not happy, nobody's happy." I like to add an extra piece to this: "When Daddy's not happy, it really doesn't matter." If mama's happy, everything goes fine. If Daddy's a grump, it's really not going to affect the atmosphere of the house. This is not an excuse for fathers to be grumps all the time, but I think it is worth acknowledging that the mother's mood is going to have more of an impact on everyone else's than the father's is. That's why I say that the mother is the glue that holds the family together.

The fourth most important job in the world is making a living. Well, the men have to do something, don't they? Now you see why I say that mothers are the most special people in the world! They've got the three hardest jobs out of the four. Thank God for prime ribs!

Regardless of whether you are a mother or a father, being a parent in general is the most important job in the world.

Raising a family is a benevolent dictatorship. It has to start out that way, but then later, the friendship can begin. You can let them vote, but when they're young you'll have to veto most of their votes. They simply don't have enough life experience yet to make many of their own decisions, and this is exactly why parents exist.

So how do you know when the dictatorship has ended, and the friendship can begin? You'll know when you hear your child say, "Shut the door, Daddy! You're letting the heat out!" You'll know then that their first signs of wisdom are finally coming out. When you think you know everything, it means you know nothing. When you finally realize you know very little and never will—again, the first signs of wisdom are beginning to show.

A Dash Between Two Dates

Life is nothing but a dash between two dates, and if you don't believe it, go look at a tombstone.

You have a window of about eleven years in which to impact your children. After eleven years, they start wanting to be with their friends instead of their parents. They may not be moving out of the house yet, but they no longer want to hold your hand and be with you all the time. This is, of course, natural, so don't let it hurt your feelings. However, this is why it is so important to make those first eleven years of their life count. After all, there is only one thing worse than your children leaving home: your children not leaving home.

They call it the terrible two's because that is the time when your children physically wear you out. But when they get to be teenagers, they don't just physically wear you out, they mentally wear you out. You'll start to wish the terrible twos were back again. The early years pass by so quickly.

When my daughter was about twelve years old, I realized she was probably about to start being interested in boys. So I decided I ought to give her some training so that she could be prepared. I called her on the phone, and I made a date with her.

In preparation for this "date", I taught her how to ask a question that cannot be answered with simply "yes" or "no". I did this so that she would know how to carry on a real conversation with someone on a date. Often the first thing you worry about when you have a date coming up is, "What are we going to talk about?" Well, you can think of a question to initiate conversation, but if it can be answered with a one-word response like "yes" or "no", the conversation won't go anywhere and you've just got yourself into another uncomfortable situation. If you ask someone something like, "What is your favorite sport? What do you like about it? When was the last time you got to play it?" then you've got a real conversation.

The day of our date, I sent her a flower. When it was time, I went to the front door and picked her up. When we got into the car, I held the door for her. Throughout the whole date, I just stayed silent. I wanted her to learn to initiate the conversation rather than waiting for me to.

We did this two or three times, and she began to get less nervous about initiating conversation. So then I called her best friend's dad and scheduled a double date with him and his daughter. We went out to a fancy restaurant and had a great time. I still treasure these memories to this day. We still talk about how they gave us sherbet after our salad so that we could "cleanse our palate". As simple as this may seem, it is special experiences like this one that that stand out in my memory as I think back on the time I spent with my children growing up.

I often hear people saying they are too busy to spend time with their children. "Too busy" is an overused phrase. I think people just say this because it makes them feel important.

People will make time for the things that are important to them, no matter how busy they are.

One way that I tried to carve out intentional time to spend with my children was that I would take each of my children out for breakfast every single week, for some one on one time. I took one child on Mondays and one on Fridays, and I did it every week for twelve years—from first grade through twelfth grade. We went to Krystal every single time. Since this was something that I made a part of my weekly schedule, it wasn't difficult to keep up. That time together really adds up over twelve years.

We like to throw around the phrase "quality time", but what is it that makes quality time "quality"? Time is quality when you are not in a hurry, and when your focus is on the person that you are with. In the case of these morning breakfast dates with my children, I was never in a hurry because it was something I was always planning on each week. I only took one child at a time to breakfast to ensure that my focus was on the person I was with. That is just one way I have been able to have regular quality time with my children.

One time, while I was at the lake, I was opening our gate by the road when I saw a man drive up in a fancy Mercedes. He appeared to be in a hurry, so I asked him what the rush was all about.

"I've got about forty-five minutes," he said, "and I need to go spend some time with my children so I can get back to work."

I looked at him with a smile and said, "If you're only spending forty-five minutes a week with your children, just so you can drive that Mercedes, you're making a big mistake."

He didn't have a response. I sure hope it made him think, though. While working to provide for your family is important, you have to make sure that you don't let your career become your god. Some people say they have to work to make ends meet, but sometimes if we are not careful, we can find ourselves making our ends too far apart. Did that man need to have that Mercedes to provide for his family? Probably not.

Spending quality time with your children is terribly important, but so is knowing how to set boundaries with them.

When your children get to be in middle school, you will start to hear them say this phrase a lot: "Everybody's doing it!" This is how they try and convince you to do what they want you to. I heard my children use this tactic a few times. When my daughter started to use it frequently, I had an idea. I decided that I was going to start myself an "Everybody Committee".

My wife and I called up the parents of about five of her best friends, and we all got together and called ourselves the Everybody Committee. Together, we made decisions about what we wanted to allow our children to do, and what we did not want them to do. That way, if our children came back with, "everybody is doing it!" then we knew differently. Because "everybody" had already met and decided what we wanted to do. I recommend communicating on a fairly regular basis with the parents of your children's friends when they get to be in middle school, so that you too can have a response to the "everybody's doing it" tactic.

As our children get older, they begin to think they know everything. On the night before my son's nineteenth birthday, I stood in front of him, put my hand on my chin as if I was thinking real hard.

"Dad," he asked me. "What are you thinking about?"

"I'm just trying to think if there's anything I need to ask you," I said. "Because when you're eighteen years old, that's the last year of your life that you know everything."

My son didn't think that was funny then, but he does now!

Always be on the lookout for learning opportunities for your children. Since the world is getting easier and easier for children, many of them simply don't know how to do anything. Whenever you find yourself fixing something or doing some other task that could be a good learning moment, bring your children alongside you, show them what you're doing, and explain as you go. Tell them why it works the way it does.

Make sure you start doing this for your kids at a young age, because when they are young, they still want to help you. Oftentimes as eager as they are to help us, we ironically don't want them to help us because it takes so long to let them do it. By the time they get old enough to where they are more capable, they don't want to help anymore. However, if you've taught them these important skills at an early age, they will likely be more eager to help out once they get older.

These educational moments can also double as great quality time. I mentioned in a previous chapter how I did this with my son Andy as we worked on houses. Any time I showed him something, I didn't just show him how to do it. I showed him why I was doing it and how it worked. He learned a lot from those days, and seeing the things that he is capable of now has been a huge blessing to me as a father.

Once, when Andy was helping me as I worked on a project, I took a moment to teach him how to drive a nail.

"Andy," I said, "When you're driving a nail, make sure you hit the nail straight on the head. If you hit it crooked, it will bend the nail."

"Daddy," he said. "Don't tell me. Show me!"

That hit me like a ton of bricks. Your children aren't just listening to what you say. They're watching what you do. I knew at that moment that I couldn't just tell my son how to live a godly life. I had to show him.

Your children are watching their mother and father as they grow up, so make sure you make that eleven-year window of impact count.

God is the Foundation

The False Trinity

I have checked the death rate thoroughly. It is still 100%. Of course, as I have said, I don't like to use the word death—I prefer to say we just change locations. And we sure are ending up in a better location than we were before. I think in Heaven, ice cream will be a vegetable, and M&M's will be diet pills (this is Bo-blical, not biblical). Eternal life is guaranteed. Preachers say all the time that if you believe in Jesus you have eternal life, but they don't say as often that if you don't believe in Jesus you still have eternal life. I think the Bible is real clear that everyone has eternal life.

Someone once said to me, "Bo, you know I'm not as religious as you are."

"Everybody has a religion," I responded. "Whatever controls your life is your religion. You just have to make sure it's the right one."

For some people, their religion is their career. For others, their religion is sports. For others, it's technology. The things that you are devoted to are your religion. That is why we have to make sure that we make Christ the center of our lives.

As Christians, we worship the holy trinity: the Father, the Son, and the Holy Spirit. Well, I think we are all born with a false trinity: me, myself, and I. And who is sitting right there at the center of the false trinity? Me. That's why we've got to kick "Me" off the throne, and put God on the throne.

I was once talking to a man who was bragging to me about his financial success. He said that his constant prayer to God was, "Lord, keep me humble."

"The prayer is not 'keep me humble'," I said. "It should be 'make me humble'." This man's pride was obvious. The only way we can stay humble and keep from putting "Me" on the throne of our lives is to keep asking God to humble us, day in and day out.

It is the Holy Spirit that gives us the ability to do things for the right reason. You have probably heard plenty of people say that they like to help people because it makes them feel good.

That may sound good on the surface, but ultimately if that is your motive, you are only doing your good deeds for yourself. Doing God's work can sometimes be very inconvenient. When you are doing God's work, you are taking care of someone other than yourself, and expecting nothing in return. As one person, we can't change the world—but we should be encouraged that we have the power to change a life through Christ, and that can last generation after generation.

The world tells us that it is things that are worth chasing in this life. We see in advertisements all the time that we deserve everything we desire: a nice car, our dream job, plenty of money. If we are able to acquire any of these things, we must remember that it's not because we deserve it, but because God has gifted us the ability to get it. Just as people with cerebral palsy didn't do anything to deserve their condition, we didn't do anything to deserve being born healthy and able.

As Christians, we must ensure that Jesus is our firm foundation. Just as we said before that Jesus must be the foundation of any healthy relationship, he must also be the foundation of any life worth living. Without him as our firm foundation, everything around us will come crashing down.

The Son Changes Everything

When the sun comes out, it changes everything. It changes darkness to light. The Bible starts with God bringing light to darkness, saying "Let there be light!" That was the first step in the creation of the universe. Light changes everything.

In the same way, when the Son comes out in us, it changes everything. Of course, when I talk about the Son, I am speaking of Jesus, the Son of God. When the Son is revealed through us, He changes everyone that we come in contact with. Just as the sun is the center of our solar system, the Son is the center of the universe—everything revolves around Him.

The fact that Jesus wants to shine through us is such a blessing. God has given us a physical piece of sunshine that we can touch with our fingers. Do you know what it's called? Teeth! A smile is a piece of sunshine that can change the course of someone's day. Just as negativity can be contagious, so can positivity. As I said before, you can change any negative to a positive, with a little creativity.

Let me tell you the details of a story I mentioned many pages back. I made a phone call recently and accidentally dialed the wrong number. The woman on the other end of the call informed me of my error and I quickly apologized.

"I'm sorry ma'am," I said with a smile in my voice. I always try to have a smile in my voice when I talk on the phone. When someone has a smile in their voice, you can feel it coming through the phone. "I apologize for bothering you."

Out of nowhere, this lady said, "Are you right with Jesus?"

I was amused at this, having only been on the phone with her for about thirty seconds. "Boy, I sure am," I said. "I asked him into my heart years ago."

Well, she was just thrilled at my response.

You will be amazed at how many people are open to talking to you about Jesus if you just initiate the conversation. It's so unbelievably easy for me to bring up Jesus in conversation now. I have done it so many times and have yet to offend anyone—in fact out of the hundreds of times I have done this, all but three people have joined in the conversation when I have initiated it. People are always encouraged to see someone who believes like they do.

In Luke 16, Jesus shares the parable commonly known as "The Rich Man and Lazarus." Lazarus was a poor man who had nothing in his time on earth, and when he died he went to Heaven. There was a rich man who had everything he ever wanted on earth, and he died and went to hell. The rich man yelled up to Lazarus and begged him to go and warn his family, so that they would not end up in torment like him. From Heaven, Abraham himself calls down to the rich man and tells him that his family has the same scriptures that everyone else has. That is their warning.

Imagine you are Lazarus, and as you are in Heaven you look down and see your next door neighbor in torment. The neighbor looks up to you and asks, "Why didn't you tell me?" How many people have you told about Jesus? In Matthew 5:14, Jesus says that we are the light of the world, and we know that the light changes everything. But it is not enough for us to just tell the world about Jesus. We have to show them. It's just as my son said to me when I was teaching him how to drive the nail: "Don't tell me. Show me!" As followers of Jesus, we have the responsibility and privilege to let God's light shine through us.

God Promises Peace

From first grade all the way up through high school, there were twelve days (one each year) that were the happiest days of your life: the last day of school. The reason the last day of school is so great is because you've already gotten your grade, and you know what's coming. You've passed your tests, and you know summer is just around the corner.

As Christians we can live our lives as if every day is the last day of school. In John 14, Jesus speaks to his disciples, knowing that he is going to be betrayed by Judas soon and handed over to the Romans to be crucified. In verse 27, he says, "I am leaving you with a gift—peace of mind and heart! And the peace I give isn't fragile like the peace the world gives. So don't be troubled or afraid (TLB)."

When we hear the word "peace", we often think of the absence of war or conflict. But the Bible tells us that we can have peace in the middle of a war. In 1 Corinthians 10:13, Paul assures us of this promise from God: "But remember this—the wrong desires that come into your life aren't anything new and different. Many others have faced exactly the same problems before you. And no temptation is irresistible. You can trust God to keep the temptation from becoming so strong that you can't stand up against it, for he has promised this and will do what he says (TLB)." So we know that God will not give us more than we can handle.

If we trust in God's promises, then we've already "gotten our grade", and we can live our lives as if it's always the last day of school—knowing that great things are coming. To quote Billy Graham, "Someday you will hear that Billy Graham is dead. Don't you believe a word of it. I shall be more alive than I am now. I will just have changed my address. I will have gone into the presence of God."

We know that while we will have problems in life, there is nothing we cannot handle with God. After all, problems aren't problems—they're lessons. Romans 5:3-5 tells us, "More than that we rejoice in our sufferings, knowing that suffering produces endurance. And endurance produces character and character produces hope, and hope does not disappoint us, because God's love has been poured into our hearts through the Holy Spirit which has been given to us."

My prayer for each of you is that you fully know and experience the Peace that God offers to us through Jesus Christ.

Made in the USA
Middletown, DE
07 September 2024

60531496R00062